THE DOGFATHER

THE DOGFATHER

The Ways of Graeme Hall, Britain's Best Dog Trainer, And Those Dogs

Author: Natasha Tristan

Dedication

Dedicated to Almighty.

DISCLAIMER

The information provided in this book is best prepared from our knowledge and methods of findings. We have made every effort to ensure the accuracy and reliability of the details given in this. Anyhow, the information is included "as is" without any warranty of any kind. We do not assume any responsibility or obligation for the accuracy, content, completeness, legitimacy, and reliability of the information consisted in this book.

Acknowledgments

Greatly thankful to everyone for their immense support for the release of this book.

CONTENTS

Preface

A little boy handed the biscuit he had to the puppy he saw by the roadside. Seeing it eagerly eating, he caressed its hairy head with his loving hands. As he walked away, the puppy followed him by swinging its tail as if in gratitude. The sight was mesmerizing to those standing by the roadside. Elsewhere, a man saw a dog in the distance and threw a stone at it. In a matter of seconds, a kennel of dogs leaped towards him at the speed of the wind. There were still people around, and they had the attitude that he deserved it. It's not just the difference in perspective of many people. Each has its methods of taming. When dogs show amazing phenomena in the circus, the audience welcomes them with great applause of astonishment. Don't we often think about how they can perform like that? A group of animal lovers expresses their love for them. It will understand that sincere behaviour. But not everyone will be able to bring that security under control that guards our home. Also, there are people who have the expertise to handle and train it all.

Dog training is a segment where everyone wants to be involved. The most important quality required to be a good dog trainer is patience. A good trainer can clarify their doubts and give guidance to clients with positivity and guidance. Everyone's style of speaking will be different. The dog trainers take advantage of their important quality of patience and slowly adapt to the language of dogs. So they can bring about positive changes in them. A good dog trainer can also be a good listener. They will politely ask the owners who come to them and find out the solution. A behaviour consultant or dog trainer will make clients' pets the best and understand things from their perspective and convince them. Not only animals but also their owners will be treated accordingly. In some cases, things may not be in the hands of a standard trainer, who will explain everything to the pet parent and teach them how to communicate effectively.

There are no specially designed ways to train a dog. When a person is unable to control a dog in its abrupt change, a good dog trainer will have a clear idea of what the next step should be. Apart from all this, the most important thing is to love dogs. If you approach it as just a profession without love, it will behave like an enemy in return. If we love it, it will love us too. Proof of that is the fact that it guards the house. If the dog trainer is someone who loves and cares for the dog like a friend, then there is no delay in getting a better result. Let's meet someone like that. Also let's take a look at how he handles every dog-related instance in his life or how he views it all. He has mastered the art of dog training and has imparted it to many people through various platforms and the ways in which he utilizes it can be understood by the readers through further reading.

Chapter 1: Who is Graeme Hall?

Gateway to dog training

Graeme Hall is the person who puts dogs at the top of his list of most favourites. He's one of the top dog trainers in the UK. It's a little more familiar to know him as "Dogfather" rather than his real name. Why is calling a man like this? Is everyone kidding him? Thoughts like this may suddenly come to mind when you hear this name. Channel 4 TV's *"Dogs Behaving Badly"* has exposed his inner dog lover to the world.

Through 121 training and seminars, he makes outstanding contributions in dog training, puppy training, and dog behaviour problems. He achieved the grade of a Master Dog

Trainer along with the Guild of Dog Trainer. Even as he climbed the ladder of fame as a dog trainer, he did not own one until he was forty. Because it was too late for him to realize that such an interest was ingrained in him. The presence of such a person was evident in other areas even before he set foot on the field associated with dogs. It is not clear how such a passion was born in him. He grew up in a dog – free home in Selby, Yorkshire.

After working as an executive for Weetabix Cereal Company for 21 years, his career took a dramatic turn. The pages turned to an area where he was not expecting at all. Graeme Hall, who was on gardening leave, trained as a professional trainer, and everything changed. He was a part of the corporate world and he said goodbye to that world forever and looked for the next direction. After he left there, he rested for three months. When the vehicle and he felt tired, they returned home.

It was during this time that he began to think about starting a new business. When he landed in a new scene as a new face, he thought he could experiment with being unique. That's how the business of *www.dogfather.co.uk* started.

Challenge

As the new business began to take root, a dog trainer named Graeme Hall grew up. He was quick to establish himself as a relief to dog owners across the country who came to terms with behavioural problems as well. He served with all types of dogs, from

Aberdeenshire to the Channel Islands. He carries the motto of "any dog, any age, any problem" with him as a constant companion. Sometimes he became prey for the mischief from puppies. In 2015, a client's German shepherd injured him in Worcestershire and he had to seek refuge in a hospital bed. He once shared that experience with the Press Association. That was the most terrible challenge he had ever faced. He tells others that they will go through the wounds anyway when they do this job sooner or later.

There was nothing that he did to cause the dogs to become angry or make them aggressive. It was not his style, nor did he follow the thought that it was great or clever. He also warned that sometimes the bad reaction of dogs will make your best efforts worse. That German shepherd was there for about a week. No one knew much about its past because it was rehabilitated. As soon as they took him home, the dog, who was standing around somewhere, ran up to him and bit him. He did nothing against it. He had to undergo surgery and stay in the hospital for one night. During treatment, they found that the dog had licked the tip of his nerve and the use of that hand had slowed down overall.

Love for dogs in screen also

With Channel 5's 2019 show *Dogs Behaving (Very) Badly*, his interest in dogs became known to others through the screen. The opportunity to do such a TV gig came to him because he was able to captivate everyone by participating in programs like *This Morning*.

That's why famous clients like Little Mix's Leigh-Anne were able to approach him. He always had a long-term solution to the problems that dogs have, such as barking, pulling on the lead, and eating everything. It was an event featuring the French Bulldog called Frankie. It always revolved around the feet of its owners.

Attending *This Morning*, he told its hosts that people were often misbehaved by behaving humbly. He also discussed how dogs bark at people who were sitting indoors during lockdown in the background of COVID 19. Thousands of unruly dogs lined up for training under him. His opinion is that dogs often receive messages thinking that humans are polite to them, and that is what encouraged them for leg humping. Prior to the new series of the show, he jokingly said that the French Bulldogs are one of the guiltiest breeds for becoming frisky with their lower limbs. And the first episode showed him pretending to call the intensity Frank the Frenchie.

Graeme Hall shared behavioural tips for puppies and hounds after the events of COVID 19 and the lockdown that burst out with its influence. He realized that easing lockdown controls would give dogs a different dynamic ability to hold on. As the tense situation in the world slowly cooled, many families brought their puppies back home. The dogs may not be familiar to newcomers who came there in the days when they were away from home.

Chapter 2: Behavioural tips

Graeme Hall has come up with a number of top tips in *Dogs Behaving (Very) Badly* to help hounds get confused by such a stressful, anxious feeling. He believed that training puppies was not difficult, but that human behaviour was minimal to ensure that the dog's behaviour was desirable.

Giving treats to create intimacy

Can you give treats? Then the dogs will show good behaviour. How does this tendency affect them?

When visitors come to the house months or days later, it's a big deal for the dogs. Because it would be unexpected for them, they would not be able to get excited or absorbed in that surprise like human beings. Young people may not have deeply understood what mature, older people have seen and are familiar with, or youngsters may not have had to face as much of their experience. Therefore, they may not even know how to manage many situations. Puppies are just like that. There may be fewer delivery partners around a home or any institution. But that doesn't mean there should always be visitors around. So a lot of young dogs may not have seen this before. So when all that occurs, that is, something new happens to their eyes, then it has thoughts like, 'What happens there, when people come home and shake hands with each other and share the joy?' In those skeptical views, a dog expresses its feelings in different ways. It will be more vigilant. It's sometimes through barking, or there's a classic fight situation. Dogs that have good observation and intelligence or are trained can adapt to the situation with their continuous practice.

Pets learn everything in the belief that their owners' home is theirs too. Sometimes they are anxious or scared. That fear is expressed by the fact that they put their tails down and hid. Sometimes it is accompanied by a roar of fear. Other times it can lead to beatings and fights. They want them to get out of their house. And if they are in the habit of barking at postmen, post-ladies, and delivery people, they know that if they bark, they will leave. The rest of us know that they jumped at the wrong conclusion. "No, no, they ran away because I barked", the dog kept making a terrible noise in his language. Like the compulsion of children in conflict! It tells the dog that it's good and that person will be there for a while. Hall points to an occasion. If a dog is scared, it's important to let it come out at the right time. Since the visitor is a dog lover, when he starts to pet it, he will assure them that everything is right. But when the dog sees that approach and thinks 'get away from me', it is a hard time.

Let it come out in its time. When the dog becomes brave you can give something to those visitors to give it to the dog. Graeme went on to say that it would lead to misconduct if treats were rewarded regardless of the value of the mistake in the wrong case.

The negative problem also arises when you do not want to give any treats to the dog, thinking that it will calm down when it barks because you are rewarding the misbehaviour. It's easy for them to tell it to stop barking because then they get treats. Then the dog will think so too, that he will get treats if he barks. Doesn't that feel like taking a bribe? You have to deal with those situations wisely. When that is said, there should be a positive response from our side when that naughty dog barks as if he is something big. When that happens, it recedes as if nothing had happened. Praise it when it stops barking, and then its joy will return. Also give them a treat, but timing is important there. Reward should be given when good behaviour is noticed, and the weight of reward increases when you want more than any behaviour.

Anxiety of separation when away from home

Try to take a break from work at home for a few days. That is, a separation from the normal routine. Everything turns upside down. At that time, physically you feel rested and mentally refreshed. Haven't you ever felt the need for a four-legged security guard in your home like that? Occasionally shift its bed to different rooms. Another benefit of doing so is that every corner of your home will become familiar with it and help you in the necessary steps. So it becomes accustomed to such an idea on its own. Then if there is any problem it will be okay.

You need to create the atmosphere for separation in your own home. Show that you do not have to stand on top of each other and that you can be quite independent.

The next step is to leave home and return. But there's a minor mistake everyone makes. That is, they go down to the supermarket. They will push there for an hour. It is feared that the dog may have a problem and anxiety during that short interval. They scratch the carpet or the door and make a noise. So they try to inform the dogs of their arrival. This is a common sight. So in the first instance it is better to pay attention without going for an hour. After leaving for a minute or two, come back and see what you got. Then do it in small increments. But often Graeme and the team try to overtake the dog. Then he will go and come back and do many repetitions of it. It didn't feel like a big deal to him, it just felt good.

As described earlier, if one pays close attention, they can find many similarities between dogs and humans. You will want to do it a lot more, because once they do, a new habit will not form, and you will have to do it ten or a hundred times. Then you make or arrange time for your needs. Different feelings of a dog can be understood by a dog lover or a dog trainer by looking at it carefully. Like adults staring at children who are lying. The biggest fear in separation anxiety is fear itself. Dog owners are worried about that too. Dogs understand this and will notice the stress on your face and gestures on your body. So when the first time you go out of the house and it looks like a big problem on your face, the dog will think differently. The dog thinks that it was fine until he saw the family, and if they are really anxious when it seems that they are anxious, it will be anxious too. So even if you think so, the trick is that you put them out for their sake. The dog guesses that it means something is wrong dear, I'll be back. Graeme Hall concludes that you should not allow your fears to dissipate.

Growth from pups to dogs

Teenage is a period in which dogs experience the differences in life as humans. When it comes to the challenging nature of a puppy's life, it can reach heights and become a bit 'nippy' with its mouth, it is the time when many owners avoid keeping them. They go through this phase for about four or five months. At that stage, they seem to forget everything that was taught. And they do not listen. They are like the teenage kids at that time. They forgot everything around them or everything that has happened before. They fall into a temporary magical world. One study proved this to be true. At that particular time, waves of unrest burn in the owners. But if you stick to it, the good news is that as teens become adults, it slows down and adjusts itself.

It can be likened to a human and a dog living environment that is almost similar. This is a context in which, in old age, when the beauty of human beings is ruined and their skin is wrinkled, they are often seen abandoned in old age homes or elsewhere. Similarly, many dogs that have lost the beauty of teens and little age can be seen lying on the sidewalks or wandering around.

During that adolescent period, many of the abandoned dogs became dependent on rescue shelters. Because the masters are blaming themselves that it is going wrong and that this dog needs more that it can give them. But later it turns out that they would have been right. The fact that not only humans but also animals need energy boosters with age and that they can be safe only through them is too late to realize those synonyms of selfishness. If you have a teenage dog, you will not be your own, it's quite normal, and will move with the flow of time.

'Dogfather' Graeme Hall shared these 2,3 ways as behavioural tips for pups and hounds after lockdown.

Canines along with humans

Graeme Hall revealed how to prevent a dog from having an affair with someone's legs.

People are very polite but it is their reactions that make it worse. In the case of French Bulldogs, they like to greet people in that way. Doing so is a natural instinct. The main problem for him is that everyone is polite. The dog does the same. When a little baby sees strangers around him and cuddles him, it shows the discomfort of not being acquainted at first. When they interact with the baby for a few moments and become mingled, they naturally close. Likewise, in the excitement of seeing a tiny tot, it will be scary when you go to pick him up right away. When those faces become familiar, he will go into their hands. The same goes for dogs. At first they stay away from the stranger, then, when the humans approach it politely and feed it, they roam around under their feet with gratitude and love for them. When someone says words like “hello” to it, they act like they love it too. All these are the details that Graeme Hall told the hosts in the show’s series about what he learned while training dogs.

To the question of how to solve that embarrassing problem, his answer was that the best approach is to ignore it. There is a limit to how much they can ignore, and it is a super-charged way to get attention. He thought that reducing dog training to a single thing would be the best moment to be rewarded. He jokingly said that he trains 20 percent dogs and 80 per cent humans while he helps naughty dogs. It is best to teach dogs at an early age. The more time one has available for them, the better it will rain on them. If a person has a small puppy, it would be better to get basic training to understand things.

In his opinion, the behaviour of dogs was significantly affected by the lockdown associated with Corona disease. When strangers arrive at the front door when its owners are not at home, it barks at them and expresses its strangeness. At the same time if there is a puppy in the house the house owners will probably never know if anyone has come to their house in their absence. Or if someone ignores the presence of the dog in the house, and gets there at the door, they will run away with the power of its barking. Pride will show in its eyes that it was his voice that drove them away. I was glad to get rid of them because of his bark. He advised the owners that when bringing new people home, they should gently introduce the dog to visitors. It would be nice to be able to keep such a bond with each other, and such introductions will keep that in mind and refresh the acquaintance when they see them later. Although he identified his area too late, his skill in getting close with canines is commendable, and Graeme Hall was a man who never even dreamed of becoming a dog trainer. He even owned a dog for the first time when he was in his forties. In the early 2000's, he picked up a Rottweiler puppy named Axel as his favourite. As mentioned earlier, this was his time working as an operations manager in Northampton. His friendship with the canines through the Axel was about to begin. Those moments he was on beautiful levels of enjoyment. With that he said goodbye to his job at Weetabix. He made a transformation of himself to work for dogs. Thus, his services as 'The Dogfather' were advertised in local newspapers. He experienced every moment of it with fulfilment. He sighed that he had arrived at the proper space, albeit late. Someone to take care of and solve dogs' problems! Gradually he took the knowledge in it to heart. He became skilled at it. He proved his prowess in a short period of time. He successfully completed the puppy and adult dog class for 20 dogs in just one night. Surprisingly, it was less than a year before he entered the field. He has been criticized for not having all the formal qualifications, but he did not listen. He silenced it all with his victory.

In his observations, issues such as dog aggression, pulling on lead, dog recall, toilet training, dogs jumping up, excessive barking, etc. are commonly affecting dogs. He says you need to first understand why your dog is behaving like that. When you think of it as a member of the household, it is easy to see why it changes so quickly. Those who are attached to it will understand the meaning of each of its expressions. For those who love and own a dog, listening to the dog expert's advice from time to time will make things clearer. Find out how dogs think from your constant observation, at least of your dog. Everyone should be caring leaders for dogs. An action plan should be formulated to get a good result.

Chapter 3: No, don't!

Graeme Hall, one of the best dog trainers in the UK, has been told how not to train a dog. Let's start by saying from rewarding behaviour that is dropped above.

No promises

Do not reward bad behaviour, even if it is accidental. Little children behave like that but parents do not give any more gifts thinking that they should not worry. But there are some who give it. The evil of giving that is like adding fertilizer to the tendency of them to repeat that mistake, at that time they cannot be convinced that what they have done is wrong or rectify it. The same thing is happening here. The first example that

Graeme shows is one that happens all the time. When the kindred reach home after work, the pet dogs that used to be moody will jump up quickly. If family members perform joyous performances to show that they are happy to see him before entering the door of the house and praise it as a "good boy", the sadness of blindness in him will disappear. Then he will have happiness and he will think that if he jumps he will get attention. He will try it more times. This is a common occurrence everywhere. But Graeme Hall says not to do so.

If you don't want a dog jumping up and down, don't praise your dog for jumping at you from the door. Do not reward children or pet dogs for unwanted behaviour, even if it is to avoid a problem. Give 'prize' means anything that makes the dog happy - quarrel, attention, play, treats, etc. Unexpectedly, rewarding frightening responses with hugging and beating them will hot up the reaction. Assurance is a human trait that is unnatural in dogs.

Do not overdo talking

Be a great leader by giving instructions in a few words without wasting time and energy talking too much or making too much noise. People who watch Graeme interact with dogs will understand that he does not talk much. It is human nature to speak, to stretch it, to give it many dimensions, and to make things more complicated. If man does not understand when talking to each other, the style of things or the way it is presented or the emphasis will be changed. In this method, the dogs move towards another direction without showing any resemblance to humans. There are many ways for man to present something. When it comes to dogs, when you ask them to sit down, if they do not obey, the tone of your voice will naturally change. Even words in an attempt to help you understand it will not work. It then confuses him.

When we go to parks, we can hear someone asking dogs to sit... sit... When the masters see the end of endurance, they lose patience and raise their voice to it and say to them "Will you sit down!!" The more they repeat, the more stress and hysteria grow in them. Such a way you will also learn how to communicate with a 'deaf' dog. When controlling these in the right way, the methods of a good leader often come automatically as a bonus. Good leaders will always be calm and determined. They will not be frantic. A good clear command, repeating the same word replaces the bad five.

In a few words, calmly makes them understand all in the way others like, it gives a good leadership to that person, whether animal or human. When we raise our voices against animals, especially to dogs, we become more hostile to it.

What if the rules added in the affairs of dogs?

Do not comply with the rules.

As an example, he says do not allow your dog to jump off the sofa again and again. Because you can't worry about pushing them again. Graeme, a dog lover, says to think on it from your dog's side too. So how does that dog feel in that situation? When he looks at it, it jumps on the sofa and they drop him. He tries again, and they drop again. He looks around in frustration as this repeats itself. When he looks like that, he sees people around him murmuring something. It thought he could stay. Inconsistencies build paths to confusion. Accidentally, if you've tired or exhausted, or the day your temper goes wrong, you do not have to compromise on your rules. You must apply your rules in the same way as before.

Even there, the qualities of good leaders are at the forefront. Most good leaders in the world are like this. You always know where you are standing along them, that's a good thought.

Don't always put in the chains, carry them along occasionally

Seeing many pet dogs accompany the owners' morning walk with them close to their feet or in front of them like a warlord, makes way to brighten up the reddish sunrise of the dawn and helps all to start the day with a positive freshness.

Allow your dog to walk with you and never pull them behind you. When you walk with a dog with a tight chain, it will pull you with all its might. The lesson taught by Graeme Hall, who is familiar with every action of dogs, is that the method of opposition reflex is gaining strength there.

Allow the dogs in your home to sit quietly with a slack lead. In the position where your normal dog is walking, slowly begin to pull back, gradually increasing the tension force. Graeme describes the application of dynamics (here means information related to force) in these contexts. When you carefully observe the dog's reaction or subsequent movement, you will realize that it never falls backwards. Because most living beings will pull against the force exerted to stand upright. When you blow your tension away, the dog will also attain its old position and release muscle tension. Some actually move with the forward drive you created. In result, you are coaching the dog to pull against the lead. Sometimes it's hard not to, and often the dog pulls first before you get to the door. You need to acquire the skill of how to get a slow lead while walking the lead. You may need help with a few techniques to avoid triggering opposition reflexes - it may be helpful to spend some of your time and effort trying to prevent the dog from pulling. The eyes of the dog lover masters feel the warmth of comfort and satisfaction when they see the dog walking without any tugs. Maybe it's like the delight shines in the eyes of parents when seeing their babies slowly taking first steps without anyone's support.

Wait patiently, don't expect an immediate effect

Knowledge and patience are essential elements, as mentioned above, but it takes time. It is not right to set aside one or two days and nights for that. The sun and moon must change their shifts many times.

Chapter 4: Fun activities to teach new tricks

Graeme Hall one day told everyone about some fun activities that can prove owners can teach their dogs new tricks. He introduces three training ideas for interesting games that offer practical results that are easy to do at home. That way you can increase your intimacy with your pet dog and raise your favourite as one of the best dogs.

Ignore it

The first thing he recommends is the word 'give up' - practicing or purifying. Teach the dog not to steal food. It may give the dog a bad name and may even lead to animosity between people. He tells you to start with a small treat between your thumb and finger. Lay the dog and hold the treat six inches in front of its nose. It is not with the thought that it should be given to it. When the dog craves it and moves its head forward, you should say 'No' in a way that it understands. Do not let him take it. Keep doing it until he goes away. Tell him to let it go as he is going to step backwards. This is to help them understand the true meaning of 'leave it'.

Settle down

What can be done to fix and keep dogs that are not standing still? One way is to tie it. Second one is to keep it in a kennel. These two would be like enslaving it. In most places where there are pet dogs, there are people who consider them as one of the family members. Graeme shows how to keep them at night. That's where the action of 'settle down' comes into play.

When you take your dog out of the room, put two treats on his bed. Bring him back inside the room and show him the treats. Repeat this step as said earlier. Tired of that tactic, he would naturally grab his bed. When he does, he should be commended to go to bed. So he would add this term to his habits. Encourage him when he sits where you want him to settle, and then give him the second.

Patience

Patience is a must have trait for the owner or dog. Let's see how he said it can be installed on dogs. He advises you to practice Bucket Game to keep your dog patient. Show the dog that it's empty by pointing a pot or bucket back and forth. It should be an object that depends on the size of the dog. When you kneel down beside him, let him stand two feet from it. When he is calm, put two treats in the bucket, but he should not be able to take it. If you have taught him before 'leave it', this is a stage to apply it.

It's too late but good things will come to the dogs ready to wait.

Keep track of how many treats you gave him. From time to time, make sure that your dog doesn't gain weight. If any variations occur, make the necessary changes to its daily diet accordingly.

The more time you spend with your pets, the tighter the chain of that bond and the more beautiful moments you will be casting.

Graeme Hall proudly carries the title "Dogfather" along with him as a decoration or an ornament for which he trains the dogs by finding the best way because they are someone who works to keep home and country truly without selfish thoughts and without coveting rewards. He makes efforts to lead the pets and stray dogs well in his own different ideas. If these methods are practiced, those who do not like dogs or those who are scared of it can make changes in that habit. So the four-legged security guard can be brought to everyone's friends' circle through the ideas Graeme Hall suggested.

Extras

A Humble Request

Our books are intended to indulge you. If you enjoyed this book or gained any valuable information from it in any way, feel free to share your experience with us. Your contented reviews will help to boost us not only in the sales perspective but also to improve our creativity. Please leave a review at the store front where you purchased this book, and it would be greatly appreciated.

Related Books

Bob Mortimer, Vic Reeves, Their Comedy and Friendship

A journey through the life of Bob and Reeves, who mixed fun & amity in woe, joy and gave comic gifts. Grab your copy now.

https://www.amazon.com/dp/B09L5DH4BS

Dave Grohl, Melodic Nirvana of a Foo Fighter: Abridged Life Story of an American Music Legend, Dave Grohl

Feel the vibes of Dave Grohl who makes hex on instruments with bands and friends. Click for an exclusive experience.

https://www.amazon.com/dp/B09L5DXPJJ

Big Yin - Billy Connolly: Tale of Billy Connolly and the Way He Nourished His Willpower from Morbidity

Attain this book to know the tale of the survival of comic Big Yin, who bravely fought in front of ail which was sentenced that there's no cure.

https://www.amazon.com/dp/B09MNTN1VR

Can't Just Chuckle – The Richard Osman Book: Unofficial Guide to the monumental moments of The English comedian Richard Osman's Life, In Short

This quietly moving book is the quick read on the towering Richard Osman, the Pointless guy whose debut book is breaking all records. Get a copy!
https://www.amazon.com/dp/B097NJ3QML

Matthew McConaughey, Undazed and Unconfused: All rights about Matthew McConaughey

To know all about the quintessential Texan Mathew McConaughey, his quest to find the meaning of life, how he engineered his destiny-Buy the book.

https://www.amazon.com/dp/B098F9D3DF

I am Seth, Seth Rogen: The Life & Ventures of Seth Aaron Rogen

A book to make you laugh and think, a book to celebrate levity, grab a copy soon to know more about the man who made you laugh like a maniac!

https://www.amazon.com/dp/B0977M74ZT

Sinéad O'Connor, The Unofficial Biography: Sinead O'Connor's Life Story In Short

Sinead O'Connor stole Prince's song, became a star; then destroyed her career. BUY a copy NOW to read the story of the most controversial pop star.

https://www.amazon.com/dp/B098MTR4LL

Andrew McCarthy, Dwelling Down Into 80's Brat Pack Era: A Nostalgic Memoir

Hunting high and low for a nostalgia-inducing book to immerse yourself in the 80s world? Get the book to know about Andrew McCarthy, the Brat Packer.

https://www.amazon.com/dp/B096F13S1W

Being Billie: Billie Eilish, A Short Life Story

Dark, but poignantly so, like Billie Eilish's songs, this book brings you her life's trials and triumphs in a candid narration. Buy a copy now!

https://www.amazon.com/dp/B095WXTGK3

Will Power Smith: Will Smith's Way to Success

Grab your copy to be inspired by the life of Will Smith, who came from rap-acting, faced strains & won success, beaten his sad infancy & other chains.

https://www.amazon.com/dp/B09RQ6ZPNP

THE END

Printed in Great Britain
by Amazon

86813234R00038